MW00453775

JOURNAL

PETER PAUPER PRESS, INC.
WHITE PLAINS, NEW YORK

Cover illustration by Lauren Wan

Copyright © 2008
Peter Pauper Press, Inc.
202 Mamaroneck Avenue
White Plains, NY 10601
All rights reserved
ISBN 978-1-59359-485-5
Printed in China
7   6   5   4

Visit us at www.peterpauper.com